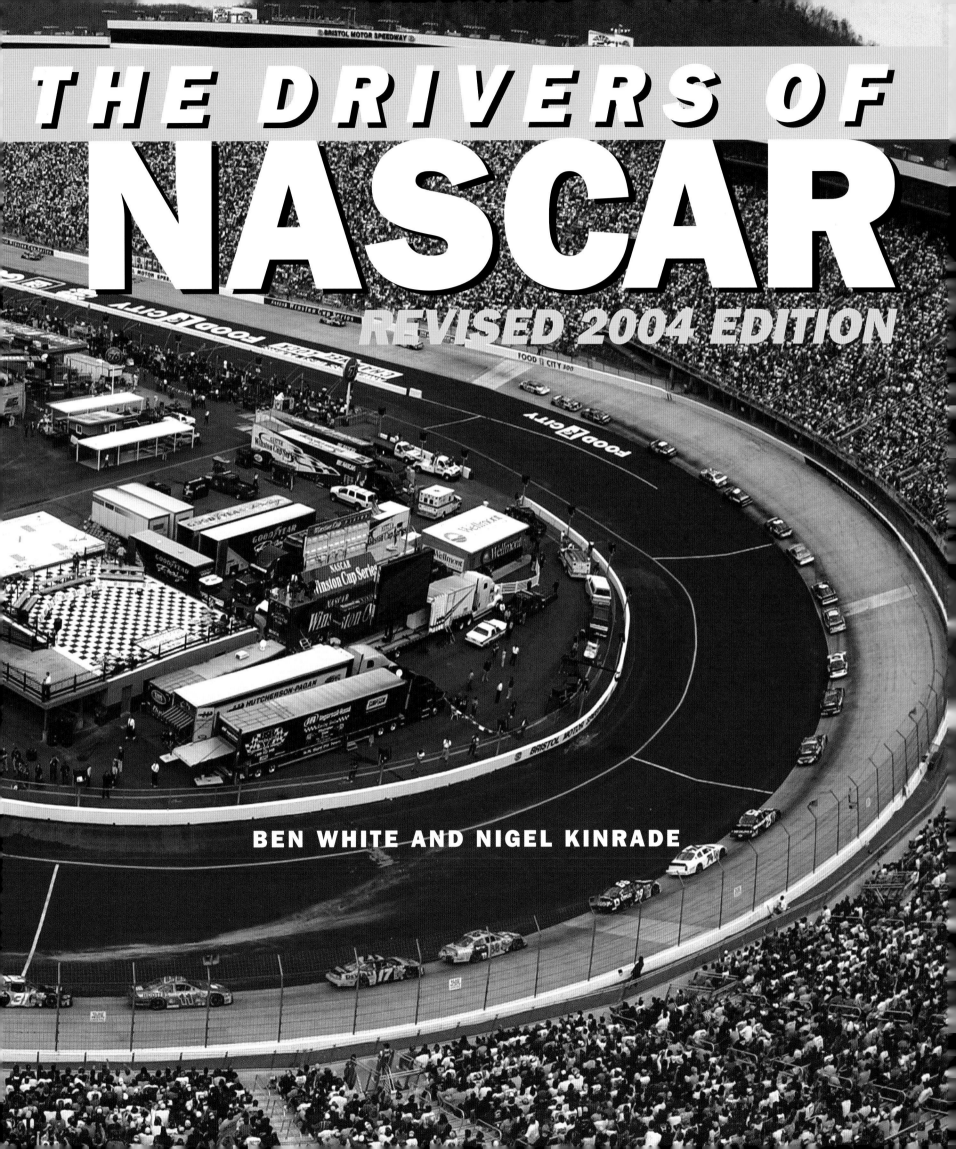

THE DRIVERS OF
NASCAR
REVISED 2004 EDITION

BEN WHITE AND NIGEL KINRADE

This edition published in 2004 by Lowe & B. Hould Publishers, an imprint of Borders, Inc., 515 East Liberty, Ann Arbor, MI 48104. Lowe & B. Hould Publishers is a trademark of Borders Properties, Inc.

First published in 2004 by MBI Publishing Company, Galtier Plaza, Suite 200, 380 Jackson Street, St. Paul, MN 55101-3885 USA

Library of Congress Cataloging-in-Publication Data Available

ISBN 0-681-04466-7

Printed in China

CONTENTS

ACKNOWLEDGMENTS

To my father, the late
Ben Newton White Jr.
Thank you, Dad, for introducing
me to the exciting world of
NASCAR Winston Cup racing.

First and foremost, I would like to thank the NASCAR Winston Cup drivers and teams featured in this book for the time they extended to me for this project, as well as past projects in my nearly 20 years of motorsports journalism. Your insight and continued friendship is most appreciated.

A tremendous thanks to Denny Darnell, Rob Goodman, and the entire staff of Sports Marketing Enterprises, R.J. Reynolds Tobacco Co., for helping to provide information both personal and professional concerning each subject featured here. They will be deeply missed, as they have completed their final year as series sponsor after 33 seasons.

Hearty thanks to Nigel Kinrade for his fantastic photographs, all of which are so central to this book. Heather Oakley and Lee Klancher of MBI Publishing Company offered tremendous contributions toward making this book a success.

As always, I'd like to thank Mark Ashenfelter, Kenny Bruce, Rob Fisher, Jon Gunn, Jeff Owens, Steve Waid, Ray Shaw, Whitney Shaw, Kirk Shaw, Art Weinstein, and Deb Williams of NASCAR Winston Cup Illustrated and NASCAR Winston Cup Scene for their continued support.

Finally, a very sincere thank you to my wife, Eva, and son, Aaron. Thank you both for your continued support of a career that has been tremendously rewarding.

—Ben White

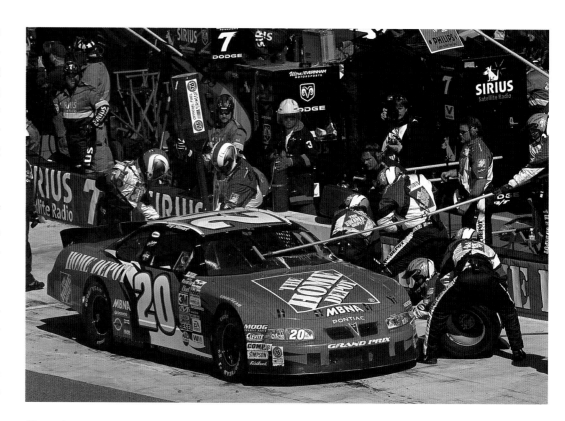

Above: Success in NASCAR Winston Cup racing requires a group effort. Just ask 2002 champion Tony Stewart, seen here getting attention from the Joe Gibbs Racing team at North Carolina Speedway in February 2002.

Below: Two NASCAR legends of the future, Jimmie Johnson and Dale Earnhardt Jr., hang loose in the garage area at Pocono Raceway in June 2002.

INTRODUCTION

Few of us get to experience the heart-pounding thrill of pushing a top-of-the-line stock car to its limits around a racetrack. Fewer still possess the elusive combination of skill, courage, and luck that it takes to be a NASCAR winner. As a result, millions of fans around the world look to these favored few as true heroes. So if fate hasn't seen fit to make us Winston Cup champions, then we should at least be able to sit down and chew the fat with our idols of the ovals.

Here we offer an up-close-and-personal look at the leading stock car drivers of our time. Some have faced both glory in the Winner's Circle and near-death encounters on the oval over lengthy, perhaps legendary, careers. Others are so young they barely look old enough to drive. Some come to the sport from veritable racing dynasties with winning pedigrees; others emerged from obscure beginnings and fought mightily just for the chance to prove themselves on the track. The highest of triumphs and lowest of disappointments can be seen in the eyes of these men and women, their actions captured by the photographs within these pages.

Wherever they came from and whatever their background, all the men and women who slide through the window into the driver's seat of a Winston Cup car are motivated by the same force: the unrelenting desire to best a rival in a turn or down a straightaway, and reach the finish line in front of the rest.

Top: Ryan Newman's No. 12 Ford ran at the head of the pack at many events in 2002, helping Newman earn the title of NASCAR Winston Cup Rookie of the Year. The win at New Hampshire International Speedway in September, shown here, was his one victory among many great showings throughout the season.

Above: Under the helmet, all drivers are created equal. Shawna Robinson is the only female driver currently on the NASCAR Winston Cup Circuit, and the first woman to complete a race in more than two decades.

Left: Jubilation! Dale Earnhardt Jr. celebrates a win at Texas Motor Speedway in 2000. The thrill of victory is what it's all about for today's great stock car drivers.

JOHNNY BENSON

10

Born:
June 27, 1963
Grand Rapids, Michigan

Height: 6-0

Weight: 180 lbs

Sponsor	**Valvoline**
Make	**Pontiac**
Crew Chief	**James Ince**
Owner	**MBV Motorsports**

Throughout his seven-year NASCAR Winston Cup career, Johnny Benson, driver of the MBV Motorsports Pontiac, has been close to victory on several occasions. To his disappointment, only one checkered flag has waved over his red, white and blue machine to date. It came on November, 3, 2002 at North Carolina Motor Speedway in Rockingham, N.C. Many times in his past, he had been in position to win, but circumstances beyond his control took him out of the mix in the closing stages.

Benson got accustomed to winning when he won the 1993 American Speed Association championship and continued on in the Busch Series, where he won Rookie of the Year honors in 1994. He followed that by winning the 1995 Busch Series championship. It was clear he could battle fiercely against the sport's biggest names. There was no question he had a bright future ahead of him.

The Michigan native began his Winston Cup career with team owner Chuck Rider in 1996 before moving on to Jack Roush in 1998 and then Tim Beverly in 2000. Nelson Bowers purchased the team 18 races into the 2000 season. It's been a union that has provided some success, but not to the level Benson would like to see.

When asked to describe his 2003 season, Benson replies, "I'd say terrible. That's the one-word answer. It's not what we expected, based on having that win at Rockingham at the end of 2002. We thought we could carry that over. We've had a few small issues to where we just haven't been as good as we would like to see. It's one of those deals."

NASCAR Winston Cup Career Statistics

Year	Races	Wins	Top 5s	Top 10s	Poles	Total Points	Final Standing	Winnings
1996	30	0	1	6	1	3,004	21st	$947,080
1997	32	0	0	8	1	3,575	11th	$1,256,457
1998	32	0	3	10	0	3,160	20th	$1,360,335
1999	34	0	0	2	0	3,012	28th	$1,567,668
2000	33	0	3	7	0	3,716	13th	$1,841,324
2001	36	0	6	14	0	4,152	11th	$2,894,903
2002	31	1	3	7	0	3,132	29th	$2,746,670
2003	36	0	2	4	0	3,448	24th	$3,411,793
Totals	264	1	18	58	2	27,199		$16,026,230

Above: Johnny Benson brings his Pontiac to a stop in the pits at Las Vegas Motor Speedway in March 2002. Left: Benson shows his serious side behind the wheel of his racecar prior to the start of the 2001 Daytona 500.

GREG BIFFLE

Born:
December 23, 1969
Vancouver, Washington

Height: 5-9

Weight: 170 lbs

16

Sponsor	Grainger
Make	Ford
Crew Chief	Doug Richert
Owner	Jack Rousch

If one were asked to describe the career of NASCAR Winston Cup driver Greg Biffle, the best definition would be that he's a talented and determined driver who can get the job done. Biffle, a native of Vancouver, Washington, has certainly wasted little time making his presence known around NASCAR circles.

Biffle progressed through the various levels of NASCAR racing before making his NASCAR Winston Cup debut in 2002. But before that huge jump, he logged championships in both the NASCAR Craftsman Truck Series in 2000 and the NASCAR Busch Series in 2002, as well as Rookie of the Year in both divisions. He also ran seven 2002 NASCAR Winston Cup events for team owners Andy Petree, Jack Roush, and Kyle Petty, gaining experience before his 2003 baptism into the most competitive form of auto racing in the world.

Biffle joined NASCAR's elite circuit in 2003 and, by July, scored a victory in the Pepsi 400 at Daytona International Speedway. The win served as a glimpse of good things to come, since a win in one's rookie season shows special talent waiting to be unleashed.

"We've worked harder than we've ever worked, trying to get our race cars where they need to be," Biffle says. "We've struggled some, but it (the win at Daytona) shows how hard these guys work and how they don't give up."

NASCAR Winston Cup Career Statistics

Year	Races	Wins	Top 5s	Top 10s	Poles	Total Points	Final Standing	Winnings
2003	35	1	3	6	0	3,696	20th	$2,410,053
Totals	35	1	3	6	0	3,696	20th	$2,410,053

Opposite Page: Greg Biffle, driver of the No. 16 Roush Racing Ford, seems to be listening to advice in 2003, his rookie season in NASCAR Winston Cup racing. Far Left: Biffle leads Joe Nemechek (25) and Morgan Shepherd (89) during a close battle for position. Left: Biffle enjoys his first career NASCAR Winston Cup victory after conserving fuel in the Pepsi 400 at Daytona International Speedway in July of 2003. Above: On several occasions, Greg Biffle placed his red and black Roush Racing Ford out front, proving his talents in the high-pressured world of NASCAR.

DAVE BLANEY

77

Born:
October 24, 1962
Hartford, Ohio

Height: 5-8

Weight: 170 lbs

Sponsor	Jasper Engines
Make	Dodge
Crew Chief	Robert Barker
Owner	Doug Bawel, Mark Wallace, Mark Harrah

When Dave Blaney first came onto stock car racing's biggest stage for one event in 1992, he was considered a true rookie in the high exposure world of NASCAR Winston Cup racing. His car, which he owned himself, had to carry a yellow rookie stripe on its rear bumper, indicating to the veterans that someone with less experience was racing with them. But he was far from being a rookie—the Hartford, Ohio native had paved the path for that long-awaited start by logging countless laps around race tracks during 10 years of open-wheel competition.

His resume was impressive, much like that of Jeff Gordon, another open-wheel standout who went on to win four NASCAR championships.

In 1984, Blaney had won Rookie of the Year honors on the All-Star Circuit of Champions sprint car series, as well as a USAC Silver Crown championship, becoming the youngest driver to win that division. Then Blaney won the World Sprint Car championship in 1988 at Hagerstown, Maryland. The following season, he posted a remarkable 76 top-five finishes in 85 events in both modified and sprint car events. Further, in 1990, he won the Pacific Coast Nationals at Ascot Speedway in California.

In 1995, he won the Knoxville Nationals, one of the biggest events of open-wheel racing. Also that year, he won the World of Outlaws championship and was named that year's Sprint Car Driver of the Year.

NASCAR Winston Cup Career Statistics

Year	Races	Wins	Top 5s	Top 10s	Poles	Total Points	Final Standing	Winnings
1992	1	0	0	0	0	--	--	$4,500
1999	5	0	0	0	0	--	51st	$212,170
2000	33	0	0	2	0	--	31st	$1,272,689
2001	36	0	0	6	0	--	22nd	$1,827,896
2002	36	0	0	5	0	--	19th	$2,978,593
2003	36	0	0	4	0	3,194	28th	$2,828,692
Totals	147	0	1	17	0	3,194		$9,124,540

Blaney places his yellow and blue Ford at the bottom of the race track in hopes of finding the fastest way around its surface.

Left: Dave Blaney, driver of Jasper Motorsports Ford, enjoys a peaceful moment in the garage area during a break in the action.

Above: Dave Blaney, driver of the Jasper Motorsports Ford, receives service from his crew during a pit stop. Usually, four tires and fuel are added in less than 20 seconds.

Below: Blaney is busy doing what he does best at speed in his familiar yellow and blue Jasper Motorsports machine.

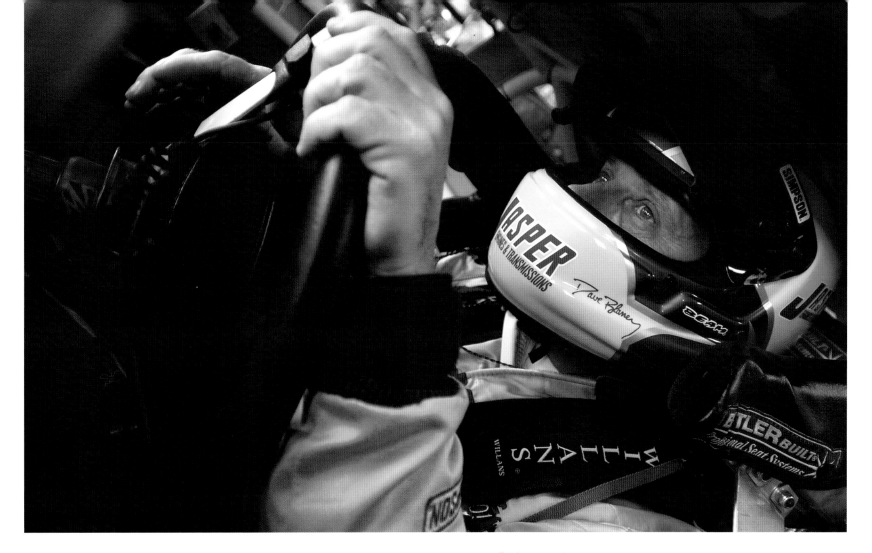

Above: Like so many times during his career, Blaney sits behind the controls of his Jasper Motorsports Ford, prepared to start his engine prior to the start of an event. Right: Blaney stands quietly, possibly anticiapting the quickest line around the race track before attempting a qualifying run.

After two seasons of finishing in the runner-up position in the World of Outlaws sprint car circuit, Blaney was given the opportunity to drive on the NASCAR Busch Series with team owner Bill Davis, winning 1 pole position in 20 starts. By the end of 1999, he had improved in his stock car driving skills to post a seventh-place finish in the NASCAR Busch Series standings, posting 5 top-5s, 12 top-10s, and 4 pole positions in 31 starts.

By 1999, Blaney once again realized the excitement of driving in NASCAR's top division, this time with Davis. His best start that season, a 4th, and best finish, a 23rd, came at Homestead, Florida.

From 2000 through 2002, Blaney improved on his points ranking from 31st 22nd to 19th. But in 2003, mechanical misfortunes and accidents, not of his making, took him out of the top-25 in points.

Still, being one of the top 43 stock car drivers in the world speaks volumes for his over-all ability. As he continues to search for that elusive first NASCAR Winston Cup victory, he involves himself in all facets of racing endeavors, which include owning Sharon Speedway in Hartford, Ohio with his family. He also fields a Sprint Car team for his brother Dale, a former NBA player with the Los Angeles Lakers.

"We've had good runs and some not so good," Blaney says. "This is a great race team and I feel we're making progress toward some real good finishes."

Above: Busch's Taurus sports a special paint scheme for his victorious run in the final event of the 2002 Winston Cup season, at Homestead, Florida, in November. Below Left: Ready for battle behind a colorful helmet, Busch awaits the command to fire his engine at Dover, Delaware. Below Right: Busch rightly enjoys his first career Winston Cup winner's trophy, earned at Bristol Motor Speedway in March 2002.

RICKY CRAVEN

32

Born:
May 24, 1966
Newburgh, Maine

Height: 5-9

Weight: 165 lbs

Sponsor	Tide
Make	Ford
Crew Chief	Scott Miller
Owner	Cal Wells

Spot a Winston Cup competitor sporting an orange-and-white uniform and a huge smile on his face, it's a good bet you're looking at Ricky Craven, driver of the PPI Motorsports Ford. Since winning his first Winston Cup race in October 2001, Craven has not been able to hide those pearly whites. Add to that win list a very impressive and popular victory at Darlington, South Carolina in March of 2003 over fellow competitor Kurt Busch. At the conclusion of that event, Craven emerged the winner only after trading paint on several occasions with Busch in the closing laps and being pushed across the start/finish line after the two collided. It is one event that will go down in Darlington history as one of the best in the track's 52-year existence.

The native of Bangor, Maine, likes what he sees these days in a career that has been revitalized with a team owned by Cal Wells. His cars are good. His team is good. Everyone seems to be mentioning Craven's name as the driver to beat in events on the Winston Cup schedule, especially at New Hampshire International Raceway, a track Craven considers his home turf. He has finally found a bit of stability in a personal racing venture that has seen its fair share of turbulence over its 11 years. One needs to look back at Craven's past to truly appreciate his present role with the Wells team.

Craven drove one event for Dick Moroso in 1991, 62 events for owner Larry Hedrick in 1995 and 1996, and then moved over to the prominent Charlotte-based Hendrick Motorsports and team owner Rick Hendrick, for whom he competed in 38 races. A couple of hard crashes with Hedrick's operation in 1996 and Hendrick in 1997 caused some head injuries that heavily influenced Craven's ability behind the controls. After Craven completed only four events in 1998, doctors determined that he was suffering from post-concussion syndrome, a side

NASCAR Winston Cup Career Statistics

Year	Races	Wins	Top 5s	Top 10s	Poles	Total Points	Final Standing	Winnings
1991	1	0	0	0	0	61	--	$3,750
1995	31	0	0	4	0	2,883	24th	$597,054
1996	31	0	3	5	2	3,078	20th	$941,959
1997	30	0	4	7	0	3,108	19th	$1,259,550
1998	11	0	0	1	1	907	46th	$527,875
1999	24	0	0	0	0	1,513	41st	$853,835
2000	16	0	0	0	0	1,175	44th	$636,562
2001	36	1	4	7	1	3,379	21st	$1,996,981
2002	36	0	3	9	2	3,888	15th	$2,493,720
2003	36	1	3	8	0	3,334	27th	$3,116,211
Totals	252	1	17	41	6	23,326		$12,427,497

Ricky Craven puts his PPI Motorsports Ford to the test at North Carolina Speedway at Rockingham in February 2001.

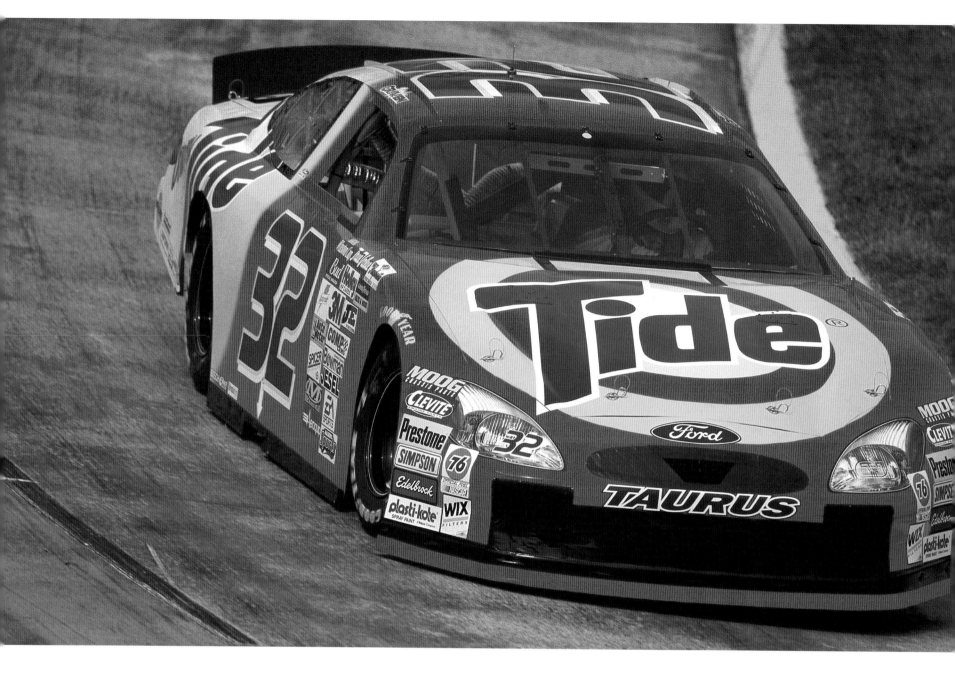

Above: Craven glides along on the low side of Martinsville's near-flat turns in April 2001. Right: Craven displays his first official winner's trophy after his victory at Martinsville in 2001. Below: Looking a bit tired after a long day at Phoenix International Raceway late in the 2001 season, Craven finished well back after being taken out in an accident not of his making.

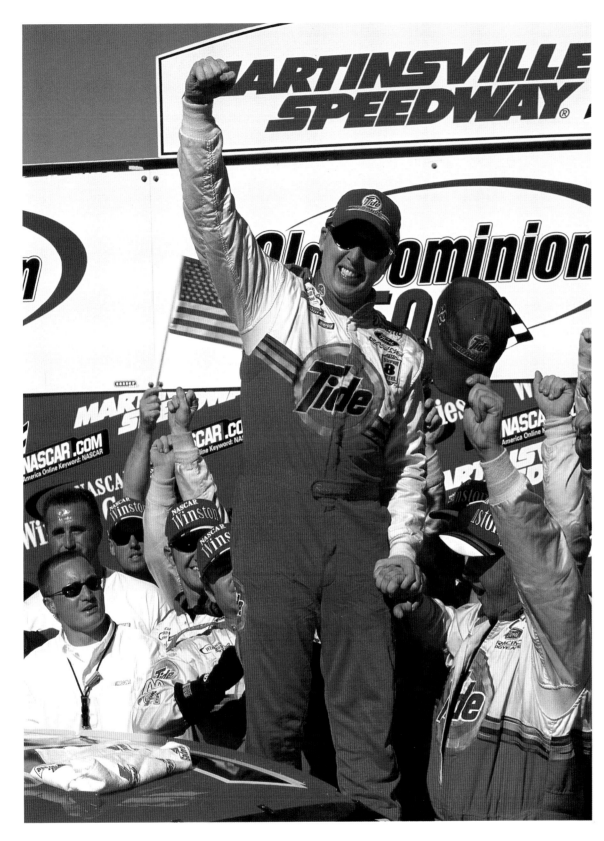

effect from the terrible spill he took in a multi-car crash at Talladega and a crash during a practice session at Texas. From there, many months of recuperation passed as he tried desperately to keep his driving hopes alive.

Craven managed to run three events late in the 1998 season with Nelson Bowers, and 24 total events for Scott Barbour and Hal Hicks in 1999. Unfortunately, the strong finishes simply didn't come. So when Cal Wells cut driver Scott Sharp from his program and tapped Craven to fill the void, it was the break Craven had been searching for his entire career.

Since joining Wells, he has been victorious twice, once at Martinsville in 2002, but he is quick to say his most memorable win was that famed event at Darlington early in 2003.

"A lot of fans I meet, that finish (at Darlington) is the first thing they mention," Craven says. "I'm really proud that I was a part of something that some people say will go down in the history books, but it's not something I constantly dwell on. In this business, you can't afford to."

Craven admits the Darlington win may someday become a cornerstone of his career.

"I don't think it will really sink in or that I'll reflect on that win until after I'm finished with racing," Craven says. "I think it will be really neat to be able to show the tape of that win to my grandkids and let them see what their grandpa used to do for a living."

DALE EARNHARDT JR.

8

Born:
October 10, 1974
Kannapolis, North Carolina

Height: 6-0

Weight: 165 lbs

Sponsor	**Budweiser**
Make	**Chevrolet**
Crew Chief	**Tony Eury Jr.**
Owner	**DEI**

It is true that one must possess a great deal of talent to be considered for one of NASCAR's most prestigious rides. But having the name "Earnhardt" as part of one's signature certainly doesn't hurt.

When the media scouted the new faces coming into the Winston Cup Series in 1999, it came as no surprise to find the name "Dale Earnhardt Jr." on the list of rookies. What did come as a complete surprise to everybody was that a mere two years later, Earnhardt Jr. would be the only Earnhardt on the circuit.

In the wake of the tragic death of his father at Daytona in February 2001, Earnhardt Jr. was looking to carry on the Earnhardt legacy in NASCAR's premier arena—without his famous father at his side offering advice and encouragement. Throughout the rest of that 2001 season, Earnhardt Jr. was a man everyone looked to for strength.

Early photos of Earnhardt Jr. feature him in one of the black-and-gray pit crew uniforms of the RCR Enterprises team his

NASCAR Winston Cup Career Statistics

Year	Races	Wins	Top 5s	Top 10s	Poles	Total Points	Final Standing	Winnings
1999	5	0	0	1	0	500	48th	$162,095
2000	34	2	3	5	2	3,516	16th	$2,801,880
2001	36	3	9	15	2	4,460	8th	$5,827,542
2002	36	2	11	16	2	4,270	11th	$4,570,980
2003	36	2	13	21	0	4,815	3rd	$4,923,497
Totals	147	9	36	58	6	17,561		$18,285,995

Right: Dale Earnhardt Jr. enjoys an unexpected beer shower in Victory Lane at Richmond, Virginia, in May 2000. It was his second win that season. Below: The red-and-white No. 8 Chevy has come to symbolize Dale Earnhardt Jr. as much as the black-and-silver No. 3 was made famous by his father, the late Dale Earnhardt Sr.

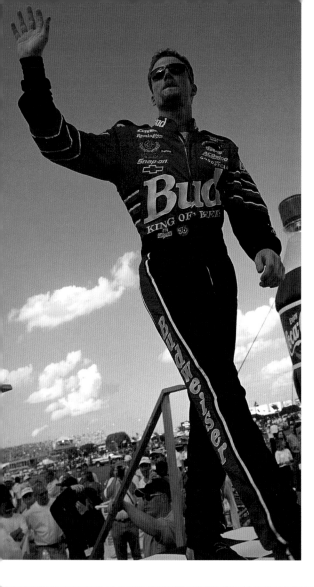

father drove for. Long before he was old enough to possess a North Carolina driver's license, Earnhardt Jr. had his sights set on becoming a racecar driver just like his dad. He was so serious about this venture that he and his brother Kerry pulled an old 1978 Chevrolet Monte Carlo from the woods and welded roll bars within its stripped interior. Worried that the car wouldn't be safe, their father decided to help his young sons and began offering racing advice. Still, he wanted them to work on their own cars to learn the mechanical side of what makes them go fast.

After a few years campaigning on the short tracks around his Mooresville, North Carolina, home, Earnhardt Jr. was ready to try his hand on the super-speedways. He earned a Busch Series ride with Dale Earnhardt Inc. in 1996. He started that first event at Myrtle Beach in 7th position and finished 14th. The powerhouse started by his late father and stepmother Teresa in 1995 came to be a racing home for Earnhardt Jr. He rewarded them with back-to-back Busch Series championships, in his first year and again in 1999.

The inevitable rise to what was known as the Winston Cup circuit came in 1999, when he drove five events. The following year he competed for Rookie of the Year honors, but fell shy to Matt Kenseth by a mere 42 points. When Earnhardt Jr. won his first career Busch Series race in his 16th start, his father was there to celebrate in Victory Lane. And when he won his first Winston Cup race in April of 2000, his father was there, too, as a competitor. The victory celebration was one to remember. Earnhardt Jr. paid homage to his father one more time by winning "The Winston" special non-points event for drivers who had won races during the previous season.

Left: With his car low and at full speed, Earnhardt Jr. does what he does best: racing in Winston Cup competition. Below: In a very short period of time, Dale Jr. established himself as a winning driver. He claimed his second straight NASCAR Busch Series title at the close of the 1999 season.

In 2001, Earnhardt Jr. achieved three emotional victories. First was the win at Daytona in July, the place of his father's death just a few months earlier. The second win came at Dover in the first NASCAR event after the September 11 terrorist attacks on New York City and Washington. The third came at Talladega, Alabama, the sight of his father's final career victory.

Many people consider Dale Earnhardt Jr. to be a viable candidate for winning a Winston Cup championship. His first three full seasons saw him finish 16th, 8th, and 11th in the point standings. In 2003, he remained in the top five in points for the majority of the season.

Even if he doesn't win a championship, he is still quite happy with himself and what he has already accomplished in his short but prosperous racing career.

"It's not important to me to have X amount of accomplishments or have so many things in the pages of NASCAR history attributed to me," Earnhardt Jr. said in NASCAR Illustrated. "I would like to be considered a good race car driver, maybe one of the better race car drivers of the past decade. I think I need more time to get the foot down there. I think it's possible that I can win some championships, but that's not as important to me as maintaining."

BILL ELLIOTT

9

Born:
October 8, 1955
Dawsonville, Georgia

Height: 6-1

Weight: 185 lbs

Sponsor	**Dodge Dealers**
Make	**Dodge**
Crew Chief	**Mike Ford**
Owner	**Ray Evernham**

ormer Winston Cup champion Bill Elliott is enjoying one last resurgence in his 26-year NASCAR career before eventually retiring to the north Georgia mountains where he was raised. A victory late in the 2001 season at Homestead, Florida—the 41st win of his career—ended a six-year winless streak. When the checkered flag fell over his Ray Evernham–owned Dodge, it silenced the critics who claimed that Elliott was simply too old to find Victory Lane again.

Elliott wasn't finished. In 2002, he won pole position at Pocono, Pennsylvania and Loudon, New Hampshire in back to back efforts and continued that good fortune with a win at Pocono and the prestigious Brickyard 400 at Indianapolis Motor Speedway the next week.

Stock car racing has been all the redhead from Georgia has ever known. He and his brothers Ernie and Dan got started early, scrounging around their father's junkyard and fixing up old cars that were perfect for racing—around the dirt roads between junk piles, that is. The boys of George and Mildred Elliott had found their calling.

With George acting as an early sponsor and financier, the fledgling race team spent summer weekends competing on small dirt tracks. The brothers eventually persuaded their father to buy a Winston Cup machine, a beat-up old Ford Torino purchased from Bobby Allison. The boys first raced the car at Rockingham, North Carolina, on February 29, 1976, with Bill finishing 33rd in his Winston Cup debut. Still, the boys felt rich with the $640 in prize money they collected.

They struggled mightily for the next few years and threatened more than once to close the doors on the team for good. Thankfully, businessman Harry Melling entered the picture, provided the Elliotts with top-notch equipment, and the wins began to come.

The first victory finally came in the last

NASCAR Winston Cup Career Statistics

Year	Races	Wins	Top 5s	Top 10s	Poles	Total Points	Final Standing	Winnings
1976	7	0	0	0	0	556	49th	$11,635
1977	10	0	0	2	0	1,002	36th	$20,575
1978	10	0	0	5	0	1,176	34th	$42,065
1979	14	0	1	5	0	1,709	28th	$57,450
1980	11	0	0	4	0	1,232	35th	$42,545
1981	13	0	1	7	1	1,442	31st	$70,320
1982	21	0	8	9	1	2,718	25th	$226,780
1983	30	1	12	22	0	4,279	3rd	$479,965
1984	30	3	13	24	4	4,377	3rd	$660,226
1985	28	11	16	18	11	4,191	2nd	$2,433,187
1986	29	2	8	16	4	3,844	4th	$1,069,142
1987	29	6	16	20	8	4,202	2nd	$1,619,210
1988	29	6	15	22	6	4,488	1st	$1,574,639
1989	29	3	8	14	2	3,774	6th	$854,570
1990	29	1	12	16	2	3,999	4th	$1,090,730
1991	29	1	6	12	2	3,535	11th	$705,605
1992	29	5	14	17	2	4,068	2nd	$1,692,381
1993	30	0	6	15	2	3,774	8th	$955,859
1994	31	1	6	12	1	3,617	10th	$936,779
1995	31	0	4	11	2	3,746	8th	$996,816
1996	24	0	0	6	0	2,627	30th	$716,506
1997	32	0	5	14	1	3,836	8th	$1,607,827
1998	32	0	0	5	0	3,305	18th	$1,618,421
1999	34	0	1	2	0	3,246	21st	$1,624,101
2000	32	0	3	7	0	3,267	21st	$2,580,823
2001	36	1	5	9	2	3,824	15th	$3,618,017
2002	36	2	6	13	4	4,158	13th	$3,753,490
2003	36	1	9	12	0	4,303	9th	$4,321,185
Totals	731	44	175	319	55	90,295		$35,380,849

Bill Elliott's red Ray Evernham Dodges proudly carry the number 9. Elliott first made that number famous in Fords owned by the late Harry Melling in the mid-1980s.

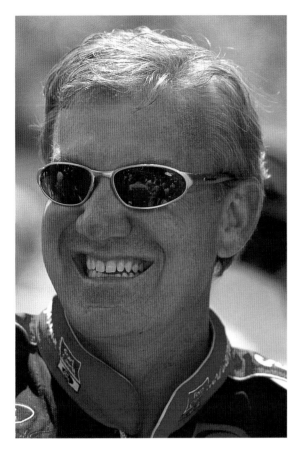

Above: Jarrett is all smiles at Pocono Raceway in this photo taken in July 2000. Right: In August of 1999, Jarrett earned one of his most prestigious victories in the Brickyard 400 at Indianapolis Motor Speedway. Below: Jarrett enjoys the moment after collecting his second career Daytona 500 trophy in February 2000. His first Daytona 500 win came in 1993.

JIMMIE JOHNSON

48

Born:
September 17, 1975
El Cajon, California

Height: 5-11

Weight: 175 lbs

Sponsor	**Lowe's Home Improvement**
Make	**Chevrolet**
Crew Chief	**Chad Knaus**
Owner	**Rick Hendrick**

NASCAR Winston Cup Career Statistics

Year	Races	Wins	Top 5s	Top 10s	Poles	Total Points	Final Standing	Winnings
2001	3	0	0	0	0	210	--	$122,320
2002	36	3	6	21	5	4,600	5th	$2,847,700
2003	36	3	14	20	2	4,932	2nd	$5,517,850
Totals	75	6	20	41	7	9,742		$8,487,870

At the start of the 2002 NASCAR Winston Cup season, new associations were formed between drivers, team owners and pit crews just as it is with any season. Among those new associations was rookie driver Jimmie Johnson and team owners Rick Hendrick and four-time NASCAR Winston Cup champion Jeff Gordon. When Johnson fired his engine for the first time during Speedweeks at Daytona in February of last year, there were no bands playing or fireworks exploding in the distance. Johnson was just another driver looking to make his mark on the ultra-competitive NASCAR Winston Cup circuit. Even though his blue and silver Chevrolet Monte Carlos carried the required rookie stripes on it's back bumper, the man behind the controls seemed anything but a competitor in his freshman season. It helped that he had Hendrick Motorsports equipment under him and Gordon, the winner of 61 Winston Cup races, offering support and advice.

Johnson showed he had enough talent to be considered for the ride. One could say Johnson came straight out of the desert to join the ranks of the NASCAR elite. From go-karts to off-road racing, he won six racing championships and three rookie of the year titles. Off-road racing deeply appealed to Johnson, but with Chevrolet's decision to cease funding for the series, he began to think of racing in other forms of motorsports. There was once a desire to drive Indy Cars, but stock cars had always been a favorite, even though it was prominent of the East coast and thousands of miles away.

He moved from his El Cajon, California home and headed east in hopes of starting the process of climbing up NASCAR's ladder. In 1998, he started three NASCAR Busch Series events and a year later, added two more to his schedule. In 2000, Johnson campaigned fulltime in the NASCAR Busch Series

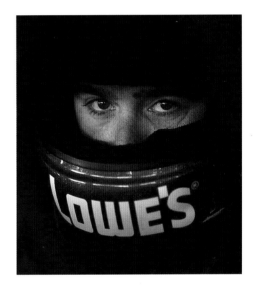

Right: Jimmie Johnson's brown eyes peer intently through his racing helmet as he prepares to race at Lowe's Motor Speedway in May 2002. Johnson earned his third pole position of the year at the 600-mile Charlotte event. Below: After just one season in Winston Cup racing, Johnson's silver-and-blue colors are well recognized around the circuit. Here he battles for position at Phoenix International Raceway in November.

in a bid for rookie honors. Even though he finished third in the rookie battle, he did finish 10th in the season-long point standings after starting 31 events. In 2001, Johnson scored his first win in a stock car in the inaugural Busch Series event at Chicagoland Speedway in Joliet, Illinois . Along with the win came four top-fives and nine top-10s and an eighth-place finish in the point standings. Hendrick and Gordon saw something in Johnson and offered him a contract as a NASCAR Winston Cup driver. The team owner and driver had so much confidence in him that they signed him before the start of the 2001 season and allowed him to fulfill his Busch Series commitment that year. The final piece of the puzzle was the hiring of Chad Knaus as the team's crew chief. Knaus had worked with Gordon as a crew member and showed he had the leadership skills to operate the race team in winning fashion. He and Johnson proved to be a strong and viable combination. In 2002, Johnson exceeded all expectations. He won three NASCAR Winston Cup events coming at Fontana, California and was twice a winner at Dover, Deleware. He logged four pole positions as well as six top-fives and 21 top-10s. Even though he fell short of Winston Cup Rookie of the Year honors to Ryan Newman, it was still a remarkable season.

Johnson was just as strong in 2003, winning races at Charlotte in May and New Hampshire in July and September, respectively. "We're building a team for the future," Johnson says. "The way this team has come together has gone past everyone's expectations. We just need to be polishing up our game and keep doing what we're doing and not put any extra pressures on ourselves. We've met all expectations at this point. Everything else is gravy. We want to gain experience so that we can be a championship threat in the years to come."

Top: Johnson celebrates his victory at Dover International Speedway in June 2002 with a smoky burnout in his Hendrick Motorsports Chevrolet. Left: Johnson's first career winner's trophy was earned at California Speedway in April.

Above: Shown here signing autographs for the fans at Indianapolis Motor Speedway in August 2002, Johnson quickly became a household name on the Winston Cup scene—and not simply for his matinee-idol good looks. Below: Johnson gets a hand from his Chad Knaus-led crew in pit row at Charlotte in May.

MATT KENSETH

17

Born:
March 10, 1972
Madison, Wisconsin

Height: 5-9

Weight: 152 lbs

Sponsor	**DeWalt**
Make	**Ford**
Crew Chief	**Robbie Reiser**
Owner	**Jack Roush**

N ow that the 2003 NASCAR season is complete, Matt Kenseth, driver of the Roush Racing Ford, the Madison, Wisconsin native has a new title to add to his list of accomplishments. He is now a champion in NASCAR competition.

Kenseth gained the points lead in March of 2003 at Las Vegas after his win there and held it for the remainder of the 36-race season. Further, he did so with numbers so far ahead of the second-place finisher it would have taken having him sit out several races for anyone to have caught up.

Kenseth's driving career began when his father bought a racecar to drive and had his son maintain it with a few friends who helped on the crew. Once Matt reached his 16th birthday, the car was turned over to him. He progressed to the ARTGO Series and became its youngest winner (besting Winston Cup driver Mark Martin for that honor).

A large part of getting into the Winston Cup arena is getting noticed. Kenseth was hired by Jack Roush for the full 2000 Winston Cup season after five races with Roush in 1999. The young driver shocked the racing community by winning the Coca-Cola World 600 at Lowe's Motor Speedway in May that year. His 14th-place finish in the points standings was good enough to bring Kenseth the Rookie of the Year award in 2000.

After a winless 2001 campaign, Kenseth quickly asserted himself at the front of the pack in 2002. He claimed victory at Rockingham, North Carolina, in the second race of the season, captured another checkered flag at Texas Motor Speedway in April, and added a third trophy to the shelf with a win at Michigan in June.

NASCAR Winston Cup Career Statistics

Year	Races	Wins	Top 5s	Top 10s	Poles	Total Points	Final Standing	Winnings
1998	1	0	0	1	0	150	--	$42,340
1999	5	0	1	1	0	434	49th	$143,561
2000	34	1	4	11	0	3,711	14th	$2,408,138
2001	36	0	4	9	0	3,982	13th	$2,565,579
2002	36	5	11	19	1	4,432	8th	$3,888,850
2003	36	1	11	25	0	5,022	1st	$4,038,124
Totals	148	7	31	66	1	17,731		$13,086,592

Kenseth also scored victories at Richmond, Virginia in September and Phoenix, Arizona in November to become the winningest driver of the season.

"We've had a tremendous season in 2003," Kenseth says in his usual quiet tone. "It's been good but it's been a really long year."

"You have to be smart about winning a championship. You don't win them by making mistakes. We got here by doing things and having things work out for us. Some people say we've been lucky but I think you have to make your own luck. I've just told our guys on the crew to go out and do the very best we can. If we do that, the points will fall right into place."

Top: Matt Kenseth drove his DeWalt-sponsored Ford to a season-high five victories in 2002.

Left: Kenseth celebrates his first career NASCAR win in Charlotte's Victory Lane after the 600-mile event there in May 2000.

BOBBY LABONTE

18

Born:
May 8, 1964
Corpus Christi, Texas

Height: 5-9

Weight: 175 lbs

Sponsor	**Interstate Batteries**
Make	**Pontiac**
Crew Chief	**Michael McSwain**
Owner	**Joe Gibbs**

Quiet and determined, Bobby Labonte, driver of the Joe Gibbs Racing Chevrolets, is clearly on top of his game. His talent is coupled with that of crew chief Michael "Fatback" McSwaim and race cars that routinely go to the front. Consistent good finishes were enjoyed at the first of the 2003 season, but the pattern was not the same at the close of the season.

From all he has accomplished, one might reason that stock car racing is what Texas native Labonte is made of. Way back in 1984, a shy and rather young Bobby could be found over and underneath the Chevrolets that were being driven by older brother Terry. That year, the elder Labonte captured his first NASCAR Winston Cup championship. While Terry was accepting the trophy and all the checks, Bobby's mental wheels began turning toward putting his own racing career in motion.

Even before Terry's glory days with team owner Billy Hagan, Bobby followed in his brother's footsteps by fielding a quarter-midget racer at the mere age of five. Bobby continued to turn wrenches for Terry through

NASCAR Winston Cup Career Statistics

Year	Races	Wins	Top 5s	Top 10s	Poles	Total Points	Final Standing	Winnings
1991	2	0	0	0	0	110	--	$8,350
1993	30	0	0	6	1	3,221	19th	$395,660
1994	31	0	1	2	0	3,038	21st	$550,305
1995	31	3	7	14	2	3,718	10th	$1,413,682
1996	31	1	5	14	4	3,590	11th	$1,475,196
1997	32	1	9	18	3	4,101	7th	$2,217,999
1998	33	2	11	18	3	4,180	6th	$2,980,052
1999	34	5	23	26	5	5,061	2nd	$4,763,615
2000	34	4	19	24	2	5,130	1st	$7,361,386
2001	36	2	9	20	1	4,561	6th	$4,786,779
2002	36	1	5	7	0	3,810	16th	$3,851,770
2003	36	2	12	17	4	4,377	8th	$4,745,258
Totals	336	21	101	166	25	44,897		$34,550,052

Left: Bobby Labonte is at speed in his Joe Gibbs Racing Pontiac at Las Vegas in March 2002.

Right: Labonte enjoys a quiet moment while at Daytona in October 1998.

the 1986 season, but the following year he began his own Late Model Sportsman career, where he secured a track championship at Caraway Speedway with 12 victories and 7 pole positions in 23 races.

By 1990, Bobby Labonte's name was stenciled on the rooflines of the Busch Series Chevrolets he had sitting at his Trinity, North Carolina shop. He finished fourth in the season-long point standings that year, and came back in 1991 to win the NASCAR Busch Series championship. Obviously with that kind of success, there was no question Labonte was going to make a career of Winston Cup racing.

Early on, Bobby relied heavily on Terry for advice about which teams to sign with. There were times when Terry saved Bobby from

Above: Labonte enjoys a taste of victory at Pocono International Raceway in 1999. It was one of a career-high five wins that season. Below: The intensity can be seen in Labonte's eyes as he awaits the start of a race at Richmond in September 2000.

locking himself into teams that weren't championship caliber. By 1993, he found a home with Bill Davis Racing but lost Rookie of the Year honors to future Winston Cup champion Jeff Gordon. Having finished 19th and 21st in the point standings in his first two full seasons, Labonte was happy to take the ride with Joe Gibbs Racing when Dale Jarrett vacated the spot to join Robert Yates in 1995. Labonte won three races that season and set the stage for good things ahead. Since the beginning of Labonte's union with the former coach of the NFL Washington Redskins, record-breaking performances have been the standard for the team from Huntersville, North Carolina.

Labonte finished a strong second in the 1999 point standings and came back to win his own NASCAR Winston Cup championship in 2000. He collected 4 victories, including a win in the prestigious Brickyard 400, in his title year.

The 2003 season lacked consistency but Labonte is determined to get that back.

"We've had some great runs in 2003 and that's the ones I like to dwell on, not the ones we have fallen a bit short," Labonte says.

Right: Labonte proudly displays his Winston Cup championship trophy after clinching the title at Homestead, Florida, in November 2000. Below: Labonte's crew services the lime-green Pontiac at Talladega. Labonte is always a threat to win on the superspeedways.

TERRY LABONTE

5

Born:
November 16, 1956
Corpus Christi, Texas

Height: 5-10

Weight: 165 lbs

Sponsor	**Kellogg's**
Make	**Chevrolet**
Crew Chief	**Jim Long**
Owner	**Rick Hendrick**

On August 31, 2003, Terry Labonte, driver of the Hendrick Motorsports Chevrolet, enjoyed a long-awaited celebration in his favorite place—victory lane. It had been 156 races since Labonte could make that claim, but with only 33 laps remaining in the prestigious Southern 500, he took the lead and held it until he crossed under the checkered flag.

A two-time NASCAR Winston Cup champion, Labonte has performed on a variety of track configurations, but he would admit his career of late has been a roller-coaster ride. Still, after 23 years of highs and lows, the 45-year-old Texan still challenges the young guns in the drive for another championship.

Labonte's career began when team owner Billy Hagan picked him to drive his Winston Cup cars when Terry was only 22 years old and working as a crew member for Hagan. Labonte took over for Dick May in a race at Dover, Delaware, in September and brought Hagan's No. 92 Chevy home 10th. He also started five events in 1978, finishing in the top 10 three times, including a fourth place at Darlington Raceway in South Carolina, in his first career Winston Cup start. The Texas oilman had found his star. Although seat time was what Labonte needed most, sharing races with May allowed him to keep his rookie status for the following season.

Labonte and Hagan ditched the No. 92 for No. 44 at the start of the 1979 season, and solid, consistent finishes followed. Labonte made 31 starts that year and netted a 10th-place finish in the Winston Cup point standings. He fell just a few spots

NASCAR Winston Cup Career Statistics

Year	Races	Wins	Top 5s	Top 10s	Poles	Total Points	Final Standing	Winnings
1978	5	0	1	3	0	659	39th	$20,545
1979	31	0	2	13	0	3,615	10th	$130,057
1980	31	1	6	16	0	3,766	8th	$215,889
1981	31	0	8	17	2	4,052	4th	$334,987
1982	30	0	17	21	2	4,211	3rd	$363,970
1983	30	1	11	20	3	4,004	5th	$362,790
1984	30	2	17	24	2	4,508	1st	$713,010
1985	28	1	8	17	4	3,683	7th	$694,510
1986	29	1	5	10	1	3,473	12th	$522,235
1987	29	1	13	22	4	4,002	3rd	$825,369
1988	29	1	11	18	1	4,007	4th	$950,781
1989	29	2	9	11	0	3,564	10th	$704,806
1990	29	0	4	9	0	3,371	15th	$450,230
1991	29	0	1	7	1	3,024	18th	$348,898
1992	29	0	4	16	0	3,674	8th	$600,381
1993	30	0	0	10	0	3,280	18th	$531,717
1994	31	3	6	14	0	3,876	7th	$1,125,921
1995	31	3	14	17	1	4,146	6th	$1,558,659
1996	31	2	21	24	4	4,657	1st	$4,030,648
1997	32	1	8	20	0	4,177	6th	$2,270,144
1998	33	1	5	15	0	3,901	9th	$2,054,163
1999	34	1	1	7	0	3,580	12th	$2,475,365
2000	32	0	3	6	1	3,433	17th	$2,239,716
2001	36	0	1	3	0	3,280	23rd	$3,011,901
2002	36	0	1	4	0	3,417	24th	$3,143,990
2003	36	1	4	9	1	4,162	10th	$3,643,695
Totals	781	22	181	353	27	95,522		$33,324,377

During the 2001 Daytona 500, Terry Labonte found himself in a rather intense battle with teammate Jeff Gordon (No. 24) and Rusty Wallace (No. 2).

2001, when Penske Racing released Mayfield from his contract. From that day until the start of Speedweek 2002 that kicked off the new season, Mayfield sat on the sidelines waiting for a new ride. Finally, Evernham Motorsports came along, and a new relationship was formed.

He had not won a race with Evernham through the first 30 events of 2003 and received a great deal of criticism for not finding victory lane with such a stout organization. Mayfield, however, came very close with second-place finishes at Richmond, Virginia and Loudon, New Hampshire in the month of September. The late-season performances served as evidence things were finally coming together.

In post-race interviews at Richmond, Mayfield said, "This shows the potential (of the team) is there. These guys gave me what I needed and that's all I've ever asked for. We had a great run. It's pretty cool to know where we came from-both tonight and this season."

Above: Mayfield anticipates the start of the Winston Cup event at Las Vegas in March 2001. Left: Mayfield waves to the crowd during pre-race ceremonies prior to the start of the 600-mile event at Charlotte in May 2000.

JAMIE McMURRAY
42

Born:
June 3, 1976
Joplin, Missouri

Height: 5-6

Weight: 145 lbs

Sponsor	**Havoline**
Make	**Dodge**
Crew Chief	**Donnie Wingo**
Owner	**Chip Ganassi and Felix Sabates**

NASCAR Winston Cup Career Statistics

Year	Races	Wins	Top 5s	Top 10s	Poles	Total Points	Final Standing	Winnings
2003	36	0	5	13	1	3,965	13th	$2,699,969
Total	36	0	5	13	1	3,965		$2,699,969

When Jamie McMurray emerged onto the NASCAR Winston Cup circuit in late 2002, he proved that Cinderella finishes can unfold and dreams really do come true. Of the millions of fans and the close-knit NASCAR fraternity witnessing the conclusion of the 500-mile event at Lowe's Motor Speedway on October 13, McMurray was probably the most surprised of them all at the outcome.

To set the stage, veteran driver Sterling Marlin was injured in a crash at Kansas on September 29 and could not compete for the remainder of the season after leading the point standings for 25 consecutive weeks. Team owner Chip Ganassi had had his eye on McMurray as a possible third-team driver in 2003 but had not yet presented him a contract. McMurray started his tenure with the Mooresville, North Carolina based team at Talladega, Alabama, October 6 with a 26th-place finish. Most everyone thought this was going to be another story of a "NASCAR Busch Series gets a Winston Cup ride" only to need months to prove himself. Nothing could have been further from the truth.

McMurray thanked Ganassi for having confidence in him by rolling into victory lane after a long, hard fought battle with veteran Bobby Labonte in the 500-mile event at Charlotte. He became the fifth driver to win in just his second outing and the first in NASCAR's modern era (dating back to 1971).

What makes the story more incredible in the fact McMurray had gone winless in all other NASCAR divisions but waited to take his first triumph in the biggest stock car arena of them all.

"What has happened to me over the past year is really hard to describe,"

McMurray says. "Many great things have happened and the biggest thing would be the fact I was given the opportunity to drive these Chip Ganassi race cars. It's an awesome feeling, let me tell you.

McMurray's now has his name etched on the rooflines of his own black and silver No. 42 Dodges and looks to have a promising career in Winston Cup racing. "I can't thank (team owners) Chip Ganassi and Felix Sabates enough for taking a chance on me. It's been incredible with all that's happened."

Jamie McMurray, driver of the No. 42 Chip Ganassi Racing Dodge, turns in a near flawless lap during a qualifying at Martinsville (VA.) Speedway in April of 2003.

CASEY MEARS

Born:
March 12, 1978
Bakersfield, California

Height: 5-8

Weight: 158 lbs

41

Sponsor	**Target**
Make	**Dodge**
Crew Chief	**Jimmy Elledge**
Owner	**Chip Ganassi**

Auto racing enthusiasts may notice that the name Casey Mears, driver of the Chip Ganassi Racing Dodge, seems familiar. He is the nephew of Rick Mears, a four-time winner of the Indianapolis 500. He is also the son of two-time Indianapolis 500 starter and off-road legend Roger Mears.

The younger Mears stuck with the family's tradition by winning his first feature event at Masa Marin in 1994 at the mere age of 16. From there, young Casey put together further impressive numbers.

By 2000, the speeds were getting quite a bit higher. He successfully completed his rookie test for the Indianapolis 500 in 2000. That same year, he finished third in the Indy Lights Series, scoring his first win at the Grand Prix of Houston.

No wins came to the young star in stock car racing but he did manage to gain quite a bit of experience racing against the likes of fellow teammates Jamie McMurray and

Sterling Marlin, as well as a virtual "Who's Who" of NASCAR stars.

"It hasn't gone the way we've wanted it to but its gotten better all the time," Mears says. "Anytime I've got a really good race car, something bad happens or if we have a decent car going for us, then I make a mistake or something. We just haven't put a good race together yet. Our OK races have been OK. We've haven't finished 15th, 16th, or 17th. We've had a lot of top-10s in our grasp. We just haven't finalized the deal. It's getting better as we go."

NASCAR Winston Cup Career Statistics

Year	Races	Wins	Top 5s	Top 10s	Poles	Total Points	Final Standing	Winnings
2003	36	0	0	0	0	2,638	35th	$2,639,178
Totals	36	0	0	0	0	2,638	35th	$2,639,178

Opposite Page: Casey Mears, driver of the No. 41 Chip Ganassi Racing Dodge, contemplates the job at hand during a break from driving during his rookie season in 2003. Above: Mears rests his hands on his steering wheel as he awaits the command to fire his engine during one of 36 events he entered in 2003. Left: Mears leads teammate Sterling Marlin as they battle for track position in hopes of logging one of many impressive finishes.

JERRY NADEAU

36

Born:
September 9, 1970
Danbury, Connecticut

Height: 5-6

Weight: 150 lbs

Sponsor	U.S. Army
Make	Pontiac
Crew Chief	TBD
Owner	MB2 Motorsports

The gameplan of Jerry Nadeau, driver of the MB2 Motorsports Pontiac, was to get to know his new team and put together a string of race wins and pole positions. The MB2 Motorsports of Mooresville, North Carolina was excited to have a winning driver in their stable and optimism was high. What occurred instead was a serious accident at Richmond International Raceway on May 2, 2003 that placed him on the sidelines for the majority of the 36-race season. In the months that followed, Nadeau slowly recovered from head injuries that included lesions on the brain, a fractured shoulder as well as rib and lung injuries. Like taking small steps that lead to big ones, Nadeau had to learn how to walk and talk all over again.

In happier days, Nadeau got his start as a master of karting. He won 10 World Karting Association and International Karting Foundation championships between 1984 and 1990.

When Nadeau entered the world of NASCAR Winston Cup racing in 1997, he did so on a limited schedule with team owner Richard Jackson. In 1998, former champion Bill Elliott tapped Nadeau to wheel his cars. Although little success came from that venture, team owner Rick Hendrick saw Nadeau's raw talent. He moved to Hendrick's organization in 2000 and won the season-ending Winston Cup event at Atlanta Motor Speedway.

Nadeau was released from Hendrick Motorsports rather early into the 2002 season. After a stint with Petty Enterprises, he joined MB2 Motorsports for 2003. But Nadeau only completed 10 races before his serious accident at Richmond occurred.

On September 2, Nadeau returned to the Richmond area and visited with the doctors who worked to save his life.

NASCAR Winston Cup Career Statistics

Year	Races	Wins	Top 5s	Top 10s	Poles	Total Points	Final Standing	Winnings
1997	5	0	0	0	0	287	54th	$118,545
1998	30	0	0	0	0	2,121	36th	$804,867
1999	34	0	1	2	0	2,686	34th	$1,370,229
2000	34	1	3	5	0	3,273	20th	$2,164,778
2001	36	0	4	10	0	3,675	17th	$2,507,827
2002	28	0	0	1	0	2,250	37th	$1,801,760
2003	10	0	1	1	0	844	45th	$861,628
Totals	177	1	9	19	0	15,136		$9,629,634

"It was emotional," Nadeau said of his visit. Obviously you wanted to cry, but I was trying be macho about it and hold it in.

"I think it was more emotional for them. Half of the people I didn't even remember. I think it was more emotional for them considering they haven't seen me in three months and I was almost dead when they saw me. It was more inspirational just to go there and say hello to all the doctors that basically put me back together."

Opposite Page: Jerry Nadeau, driver of the MB2 Motorsports Pontiac, seems to be studying activity in the garage area during a break in the action. Above: Nadeau pushes the throttle of his MB2 Pontiac in one of only 10 starts with the team before an accident during qualifying at Richmond International Raceway in September of 2003 sidelined his career.

JOE NEMECHEK

25

Born:
September 26, 1963
Lakeland, Florida

Height: 5-9

Weight: 185 lbs

Sponsor	**UAW-Delphi**
Make	**Chevrolet**
Crew Chief	**Peter Sospenzo**
Owner	**Rick Hendrick**

For Joe Nemechek, the rule has always been that if it goes fast, it's ready to race. From the time Joe and his late brother John were old enough to reach the pedals on their bicycles, they dreamed of becoming stars in NASCAR. Sadly, at the age of 27, John Nemechek lost his life in an accident during a NASCAR Craftsman Truck Series event in March 1997.

From an early age, Joe Nemechek has had the word "champion" associated with his name. He began racing motocross at age 13, winning more than 300 trophies in six years, before entering the realm of short-track events in his native Florida in 1987.

Never one to do anything halfway, Nemechek won Rookie of the Year honors and championships in three straight years. He went on to take the NASCAR Busch Series championship in 1992 before officially joining the NASCAR Winston Cup ranks in 1993. To date, he is a two-time winner in Winston Cup and has collected nearly $10 million in earnings.

In 2002, Nemechek joined Hendrick Motorsports, replacing Jerry Nadeau. The result late in the season showed promising results with crew chief Peter Sospenzo.

In 2003, Nemechek and Sospenzo pulled off a strong victory at Richmond, Virginia on May 3. Even so, the 10-year veteran lost his ride with Hendrick to make way for the younger NASCAR Busch Series standout Brian Vickers.

"Rick (Hendrick) is doing everything he can to help me land a good, quality ride for next year," Nemechek says. "Rick had to start pulling all the resources he could and GMAC (Vickers NASCAR Busch Series sponsor) said they'd step up. It's a great opportunity for Brian Vickers."

NASCAR Winston Cup Career Statistics

Year	Races	Wins	Top 5s	Top 10s	Poles	Total Points	Final Standing	Winnings
1993	5	0	0	0	0	389	44th	$56,580
1994	29	0	1	3	0	2,673	27th	$389,565
1995	29	0	1	4	0	2,742	28th	$428,925
1996	29	0	0	2	0	2,391	34th	$666,247
1997	30	0	0	3	2	2,754	28th	$732,194
1998	32	0	1	4	0	2,897	26th	$1,343,991
1999	34	1	1	3	3	2,956	30th	$1,634,946
2000	34	0	3	9	1	3,534	15th	$2,105,042
2001	31	1	1	4	0	2,994	28th	$2,510,723
2002	33	0	3	3	0	2,682	34th	$2,453,020
2003	36	1	2	6	0	3,426	25th	$2,560,484
Totals	322	3	13	41	6	29,438		$14,881,717

Above: Joe Nemechek took over the UAW-Delphi Chevrolet for Hendrick Motorsports in 2002.
Left: Nemechek celebrates a surprise win at New Hampshire Speedway in September 1999.

RYAN NEWMAN

Born:
December 8, 1977
South Bend, Indiana

Height: 5-11

Weight: 207 lbs

12

Sponsor
Alltel
Make
Ford
Crew Chief

Ever If Ryan Newman, driver of the Penske Racing Dodge proved anything in 2003 it was that engineers can win stock car races. The Purdue University graduate by far sealed the win category with eight wins through the Oct. 5 event at Kansas Speedway and threatened to win a few more before the season was complete.

Newman also had another impressive notation in his resume; he was also successful in the lighter, lightning fast open wheel machines.

Ever since Rick Hendrick discovered Jeff Gordon within the open-wheel Sprint Car ranks, other team owners have scoured the Sprint grids for potential future champions. When team owners Roger Penske, Don Miller, and Rusty Wallace went out looking for new talent, they discovered Ryan Newman, a 24-year-old open-wheel star who is already in the Quarter Midget Hall of Fame.

Having been named to Penske's organization carried a huge amount of clout, as Penske is known in several forms of auto racing around the world for have the best equipment, and talent, money can buy. Having the endorsement of Wallace, the 1989 NASCAR Winston Cup champion, made acceptance in the garage area a bit easier. From there, Newman would slowly gain their respect on and off the race track.

Newman graduated from Purdue University with a degree in Vehicular Structural Engineering, something that might come in handy when setting up some of the Winston Cup machines. He pulled off wins in ARCA (Automobile Racing Club of America) competition at Pocono, Kentucky Speedway, and Charlotte. He was also victorious in all three USAC divisions: midgets, sprint cars, and the Silver Bullet Series.

Newman competed in both the Winston Cup and Busch Series in 2001, and his

NASCAR Winston Cup Career Statistics

Year	Races	Wins	Top 5s	Top 10s	Poles	Total Points	Final Standing	Winnings
2000	1	0	0	0	0	40	--	$37,825
2001	7	0	2	2	1	652	49th	$465,276
2002	36	1	14	22	6	4,593	6th	$4,373,830
2003	36	8	17	22	11	4,711	6th	$4,827,377
Totals	80	9	33	46	18	9,996		$9,704,308

Right: Focus and determination put Ryan Newman alongside savvy veterans during his Rookie of the Year campaign in 2002. Below: The young Newman has quickly made a name for himself in his Penske Racing Ford. At Darlington in March 2002 he earned a fifth-place finish, one of 14 top fives on the year.

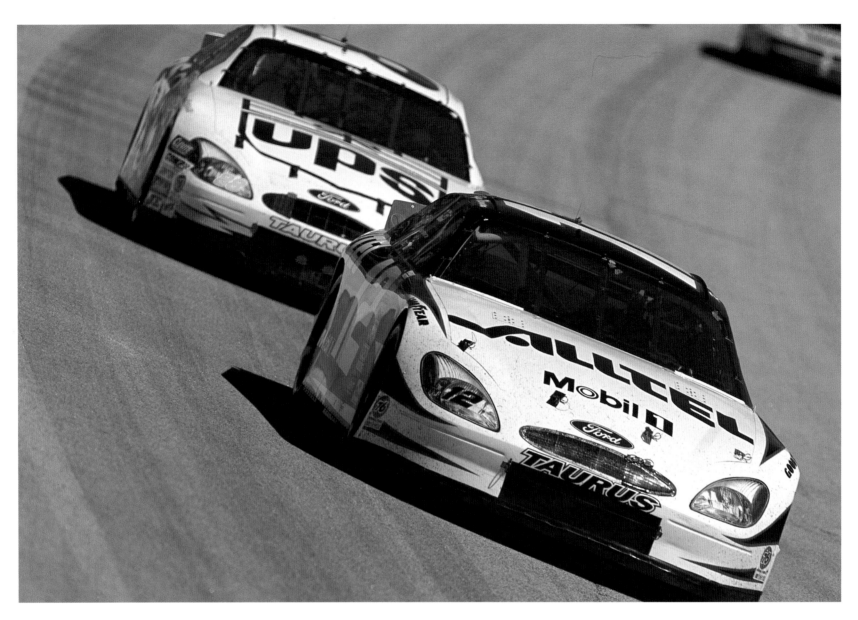

impact on the scene was almost immediate. In only his third career Winston Cup start, he scored a pole position in the 600-mile event at Charlotte. In seven starts that season, Newman kept his Penske Racing Ford up front on several occasions. He grabbed a fifth-place finish at Michigan in June, and topped that with a second-place running, behind Jeff Gordon, at Kansas Speedway's inaugural race in September.

In 2002, Newman won at Loudon, New Hampshire and collected that elusive first NASCAR Winston Cup victory. Even though weather dictated NASCAR's decision to red-flag the event in its late stages, the win was still his. So many within the sport had predicted, without a doubt, he would win Winston Cup events. Even more insiders predicted he will continue to score victories each season and establish himself as a rising superstar. All one has to do is look at his 2002 statistics of 14 top-fives and 22 top-10s to see his rise to the top is quickly developing.

Those numbers also proved to be the foundation for winning 2002 Rookie of the Year honors. After a hard-fought battle with Jimmie Johnson, driver of the Hendrick Motorsports Chevrolet, Newman's smooth-ness behind the wheel of his race cars and behind the microphone during interviews proved he had the charisma to represent NASCAR well.

In 2003, Newman certainly showed the veteran drivers how to get the job done.

"This is absolutely race team and I wouldn't have the wins I have without them. Matt Borland (crew chief) and the entire team worked hard to keep us out front and winning races."

"Our team is no different than anybody else. We've got a great bunch of guys. That to me is the difference as far as their character. Things happen to everybody. It's who can fight through it the best, and they've done a great job of doing that."

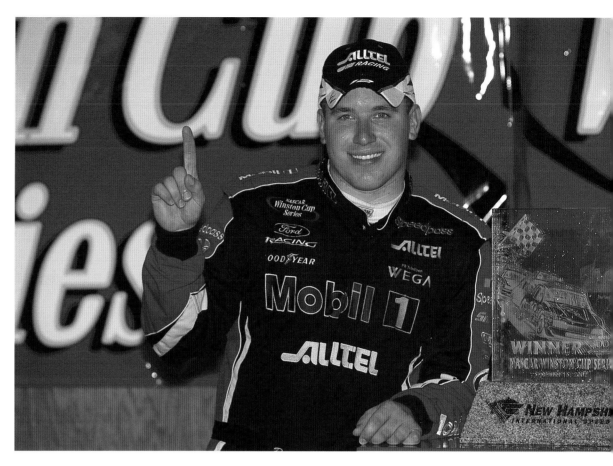

Top Left: The concentration shown on Newman's face helps explain his success on the track, where focus is essential. Above Right: Although he finished sixth in the overall standings, Newman claimed just one winner's trophy during the 2002 season. It came at New Hampshire International Speedway in September, and was the first of his young career. Below Left: Newman's rapid rise to the top made him the target of many interviewers during his stellar rookie campaign. Below Right: Newman gets service from his crew during the NAPA Auto Parts 500 at California Speedway in April 2002.

STEVE PARK

30

Born:
August 23, 1967
East Northport, New York

Height: 6-2

Weight: 190 lbs

Sponsor
AOL
Make
Chevrolet
Crew Chief

When Dale Earnhardt was looking for a driver to wheel his Chevrolets in the Busch Series for the team he was developing, Dale Earnhardt Inc., he needed a hot shoe who was young and hungry to win. He placed his confidence in Steve Park, a driver who went on to show his famous employer that he could win in Winston Cup competition as well. Park began racing in the northeastern United States, following in the footsteps of his father, Bob Park, a winning modified driver in the region for many years. Now Bob Park drives modifieds in the New York area in cars owned by his famous son, Steve.

From the ARCA division to the NASCAR Featherlite Modified Series in 1995, Steve Park put together a program good enough to finish second in the season-long points battle. When he won three times and took Rookie of the Year honors in Earnhardt's car in 1997, he was already being talked about as a promising Winston Cup star.

Since entering the Winston Cup arena in 1998, Park's career has been one of feast or famine. Before he could even get his career going, he crashed during a practice session at Atlanta Motor Speedway and suffered a severely broken leg that caused him to miss 15 of the scheduled 34 events. He came back to finish 11th at Michigan Speedway in August of that year, and again at Dover Downs a month later.

In 2000, Park broke into Victory Lane by winning at Watkins Glen, the track he considers his home track. One of Park's most special moments was having Earnhardt greet him in Victory Lane after he stood on top of his yellow and black Chevrolet.

A year later, Park seemed to be on the fast track to success. Just one week after

NASCAR Winston Cup Career Statistics

Year	Races	Wins	Top 5s	Top 10s	Poles	Owner Total Points	Final Standing	Winnings
1997	5	0	0	0	0	326	51st	$74,480
1998	17	0	0	0	0	1,322	42nd	$487,265
1999	34	0	0	5	0	3,481	14th	$1,767,690
2000	34	1	6	13	2	3,934	11th	$2,283,629
2001	24	1	5	12	0	2,859	32nd	$2,385,971
2002	32	0	0	2	0	2,694	33rd	$2,681,590
2003	35	0	1	3	2	2,923	32nd	$2,686,915
Totals	146	2	11	32	2	14,616		$9,680,625

Steve Park's yellow-and-black No. 1 machine is familiar to NASCAR fans. Here he passes the grandstands at Martinsville Speedway in April 2002.

Earnhardt lost his life on the final lap of the Daytona 500, Park scored a photo-finish victory over Bobby Labonte at Rockingham. He followed that up with 11 more top-10 finishes, including second places at Darlington, Texas, and Dover Downs.

Twenty-four races into the season, Park was sitting in 10th place in the Winston Cup point standings when he was involved in a freak accident during a Busch Series event. Crew members within the sport speculate that the steering wheel on Park's Chevrolet was not properly attached by the standard pin that secured it to the steering column. The wheel came off in his hands and with-

out control of the car, he was T-boned in the driver's side by Larry Foyt, who was moving up to his proper starting position on the inside line as a lapped car.

Park suffered head injuries in the crash, requiring many months of slow recovery. The results after the crash were not as good and he or his team had expected. Both team and driver continued to hope for future success.

Finally, by the time the circuit reached the 600-mile event at Charlotte, North Carolina in May of 2003, Park was offered a ride with powerhouse team owner Richard Childress. The union produced pole posi-

Park ponders the race ahead at Dover Downs in June 2000.

tions at Fontana, California in April and Daytona Beach in July and scored one top-five and three top-10s through Kansas. Still, the driver and team owner elected to part ways at season's end.

"I've had a great experience with RCR and Richard has been very supportive throughout our relationship," Park says. "I greatly appreciate him giving me the opportunity to drive for his organization this season," stated Park. "I feel that I am in the best physical shape I have ever been and I know that I still have a lot to look forward to as a winning driver."

Above: Suited up and ready for action, Park is focused behind the wheel of his DEI Chevrolet Monte Carlo at Darlington in September 2000. Below Left: The DEI crew works fast to keep Park's ride running smoothly. Below Right: Park studies the winding road course at Watkins Glen. In August 2000, he scored his first career Winston Cup victory there.

Then came Junior Johnson, a man known for winning races and championships. Johnson's desire for drivers to push the button, and the fact that Spencer knew no other way to race, made for a perfect pair. At the start of the 1994 Winston Cup season, Spencer immediately showed his strength at the Daytona 500, and then went on to win the Pepsi 400 there in July and the DieHard 500 at Talladega three weeks later, notching victories at the two foremost restrictor-plate tracks.

Spencer elected to return to the cars fielded by Travis Carter in 1995, but found little success. Still, the driver and team owner remained together until the end of the 2001 season.

For 2002 Spencer hooked up with Chip Ganassi and Felix Sabates, driving Dodges for the first time in his career. Spencer could only muster two top-five and six top-10s and was released from the team at the end of the season. From there, Spencer elected to join Jim Smith in 2003 and enjoyed some strong runs. Still, the final statistics didn't reflect the team's true potential.

"There have been times when we've really shown some promise in 2003 and on the other side of that, we've had our share of problems," Spencer says. "I'm certain about one thing; this is a tough race team that can win races. We're not there yet but there's still time to win one."

TONY STEWART

20

Born:
May 20, 1971
Rushville, Indiana

Height: 5-9

Weight: 170 lbs

Sponsor
Home Depot
Make
Pontiac
Crew Chief

When Tony Stewart arrived in the NASCAR Winston Cup arena to drive Pontiacs for team owner Joe Gibbs, most everyone billed him as a likely instant winner. The Indiana native had already spent many years winning races in the Open Wheel Sprint Car ranks as well as in the most elite of open-wheel arenas, the Indianapolis 500. With such tremendous talent established so early on, the gates of Victory Lane would most certainly not be padlocked long while he was around.

Stewart exceeded expectations and began his Winston Cup portfolio by breaking the record for wins by a rookie and winning the 1999 NASCAR Winston Cup Rookie of the Year. His first career victory came in his 25th start, at Richmond International Raceway in Virginia. By season's end, Stewart and his team were clicking well enough to win back-to-back races at Phoenix, Arizona, and Homestead, Florida.

Perhaps Stewart's most impressive accomplishment of 1999 was racing in both the Coca-Cola World 600 at Charlotte and the Indianapolis 500 on the same day.

NASCAR Winston Cup Career Statistics

Year	Races	Wins	Top 5s	Top 10s	Poles	Total Points	Final Standing	Winnings
1999	34	3	12	21	2	4,774	4th	$3,190,149
2000	34	6	12	23	2	4,570	6th	$3,642,348
2001	36	3	15	22	0	4,763	2nd	$4,941,463
2002	36	3	15	21	4	4,800	1st	$4,695,150
2003	36	2	12	18	1	4,549	7th	$5,227,503
Totals	176	17	66	105	9	23,456		$21,696,613

Above: Tony Stewart is set and ready for action as he awaits the start of the race at Rockingham in October 2000.

Left: Stewart's orange-and-white Pontiac is one of the most recognized rides on the Winston Cup circuit, especially after the championship run in 2002.

Above: Stewart shares a laugh with Joe Gibbs Racing teammate Bobby Labonte in the garage area at Darlington in 2000. Left: Stewart shows his anger toward Kenny Irwin after the two made contact on the track at Martinsville, Virginia, in March 1999.

After an exhaustive 1,100 miles of high-speed magic, he finished fourth in the 600 at Charlotte Motor Speedway and ninth in the 500 at Indianapolis Motor Speedway.

In 2000, many looked to Stewart to pull off the rare accomplishment of winning a Winston Cup championship the very next year after capturing rookie honors. Unfortunately, Stewart got off to a slow start in his sophomore season, ultimately finishing a respectable sixth in points, while teammate Bobby Labonte captured his first Winston Cup championship.

The next year, Tony Stewart enjoyed his best season to date. He started 2001 off with a victory in the Bud Shoot-Out, a special non-points event for pole-position winners. In June, he was a winner on the road course at Sears Point, California. He followed that performance with another victory at Richmond and also pulled off a win at the demanding high-banked short track of Bristol Motor Speedway. In the end, he finished second to Jeff Gordon in the overall championship hunt after coming on strong at the end when others suffered mechanical failures.

For the second time in his career, Stewart attempted the Charlotte-Indy double duty in 2001. He again finished strong, coming in sixth in the 500 and third in the 600 at Charlotte. He elected not to do so in 2002, knowing the championship race needed his full attention.

That year, Stewart was successful and

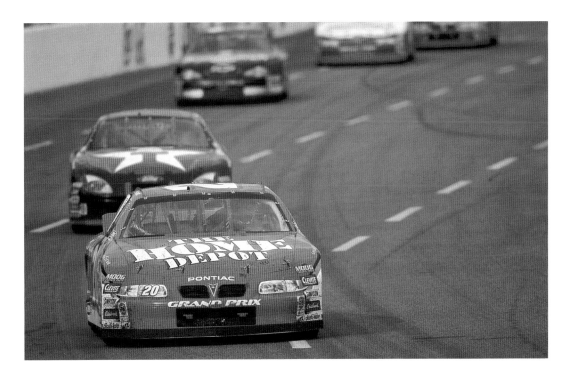

put together his first-career NASCAR Winston Cup championship with three victories, 15 top-fives and 21 top-10s in 36 starts.

For 2003, Stewart enjoyed a win at Pocono, Pennsylvania and several races where he challenged for the win but settled for top-five finishes.

"When you have a year like we did last year, we needed a lot of luck at the end of the year to help us get to where we were, and that's what happened," Stewart says. "We had some good luck happen to us.

"We went from everything being really good at the end of (2002) to things starting off good, then going South on us. Now, hopefully, it's coming back to the other side of that circle and coming full circle."

Top: Stewart leads the field at Lowe's Motor Speedway in October 2000. Even though he has yet to win at the 1.5-mile speedway, some of his best finishes have come at the Charlotte track. Above: Number 1! Stewart's victory in the MBNA America 500 at Atlanta Motor Speedway helped him down the road to a championship in 2002. Left: Stewart makes a pit stop at Las Vegas in March 2002 en route to recording another top-5 finish.

KENNY WALLACE 23

Born:
August 23, 1963
St. Louis, Missouri

Height: 5-11

Weight: 180 lbs

Sponsor
Stacker2
Make
Dodge

K enny Wallace may still be looking for that elusive first victory on the NASCAR Winston Cup circuit, but the laughs come easy for this would-be stand-up comic. While filling in as an interim driver for Dale Earnhardt Inc. in Steve Park's Chevrolets, Wallace has nothing but jokes to tell in the garage areas on the 36-race schedule. But when it comes to standing on the throttle in any of the Winston Cup or Busch Series cars he drives, it's no laughing matter.

The native of Fenton, Missouri, and younger brother of 1989 Winston Cup champion Rusty Wallace has proven that he can take a racecar to the front of the field on a Sunday afternoon. In 2002, he split his time between the top two series while Park recuperated from head injuries suffered during a Busch Series event at Darlington Raceway in September 2001.

For 11 seasons, Wallace has shown some impressive moves on the racetrack. Known as "Herman" in the garage area for the name he uses on the two-way radio during races, Wallace is always creating a stir with his hardy laugh and infectious grin.

Wallace feels good about the upcoming 2004 NASCAR season, even though this past season offered some disappointments.

"At the end of 2002, we were qualifying well and I thought we were making some pretty strong gains," Wallace says. "The 2003 season was definitely a disappointment. But it's not for the lack of effort. The 2003 season has been like the Richard Petty commercial where he says, 'You can't get upset over one bad race or one bad year.' Nothing devastating has gone bad. It's just that it hasn't been the year we were hoping for."

NASCAR Winston Cup Career Statistics

Year	Races	Wins	Top 5s	Top 10s	Poles	Total Points	Final Standing	Winnings
1990	1	0	0	0	0	85	--	$96,050
1991	5	0	0	0	0	412	44th	$58,325
1993	30	0	0	3	0	2,893	23rd	$330,325
1994	12	0	1	3	0	1,413	40th	$235,005
1995	11	0	0	0	0	875	42nd	$151,700
1996	30	0	0	2	0	2,694	28th	$457,665
1997	31	0	0	2	2	2,462	33rd	$939,001
1998	31	0	0	7	0	2,615	31st	$1,019,861
1999	34	0	3	5	0	3,210	22nd	$1,416,208
2000	34	0	1	1	0	2,877	26th	$1,723,966
2001	24	0	1	2	1	2,054	39th	$1,507,922
2002	21	0	0	1	0	1,868	39th	$1,379,800
2003	36	0	0	1	0	3,061	30th	$2,480,492
Totals	300	0	6	27	3	26,520		$11,796,320

Above: Kenny Wallace motors around the bend in his dodge. Left: Wallace waits in anticipation for the start of the race.

RUSTY WALLACE

2

Born:
August 14, 1956
Fenton, Missouri
Height: 6-0
Weight: 185 lbs

Sponsor
Miller Lite
Make
Dodge
Crew Chief

There are few drivers in any type of auto racing who have enjoyed the fan following Rusty Wallace has enjoyed. On top of his game or struggling for position, his fans are loyal, sticking by him in the best or worst of streaks.

When a bushy-haired Rusty Wallace brought a Roger Penske–owned Chevrolet to Atlanta Motor Speedway on March 16, 1980, the young Missourian wasn't supposed to have much of a chance. After all, he was a rookie competing in his first Winston Cup event. But Wallace made the most of his ride that day, mixing it up with the veterans of the sport and making it look easy. Wallace was leading with 29 laps to go when Dale Earnhardt passed him for the win. Wallace held on for second place, and the sensational debut was an indication of things to come.

Wallace won rookie honors in USAC competition in 1979 and was the 1983 ASA champion. Wallace established himself throughout the Midwest as a strong threat to win anywhere he raced, and he entered select Cup races, hungry for a ride in the big show. In his first full season in NASCAR Winston Cup racing, Wallace teamed with owner Cliff Stewart to become the 1984 Rookie of the Year. His first victory came in the 76th start of his career, on April 6, 1986, at Bristol Motor Speedway.

Within just two years Wallace was contending for the championship, finishing as

NASCAR Winston Cup Career Statistics

Year	Races	Wins	Top 5s	Top 10s	Poles	Total Points	Final Standing	Winnings
1980	2	0	1	1	0	291	--	$22,760
1981	4	0	0	1	0	399	--	$12,895
1982	3	0	0	0	0	186	--	$7,655
1983	0	0	0	0	0	0	--	$1,100
1984	30	0	2	4	0	3,316	14th	$195,927
1985	28	0	2	8	0	2,867	19th	$233,670
1986	29	2	4	16	0	3,757	6th	$557,354
1987	29	2	9	16	1	3,818	5th	$690,652
1988	29	6	19	23	2	4,464	2nd	$1,411,567
1989	29	6	13	20	4	4,176	1st	$2,247,950
1990	29	2	9	16	2	3,676	6th	$954,129
1991	29	2	9	14	2	3,582	10th	$502,073
1992	29	1	5	12	1	3,556	13th	$657,925
1993	30	10	19	21	3	4,446	2nd	$1,702,154
1994	31	8	17	20	2	4,207	3rd	$1,914,072
1995	31	2	15	19	0	4,240	5th	$1,642,837
1996	31	5	8	18	0	3,717	7th	$1,665,315
1997	32	1	8	12	1	3,598	9th	$1,705,625
1998	33	1	15	21	4	4,501	4th	$2,667,889
1999	34	1	7	16	4	4,155	8th	$2,454,050
2000	34	4	12	20	9	4,544	7th	$3,621,468
2001	36	1	8	14	0	4,481	7th	$4,788,652
2002	36	0	7	17	1	4,574	7th	$4,090,050
2003	36	0	2	12	0	3,950	14th	$3,766,744
Totals	634	54	191	321	36	80,501		$37,514,510

Always a threat to win in his Penske Racing Ford, Rusty Wallace shows his muscle at Bristol in March 2002. It was one of several top-10 finishes for the Miller Lite car.

runner-up for the 1988 Winston Cup title to Bill Elliott by only 24 points. A year later, after a season-long battle with Earnhardt, Wallace was crowned the 1989 NASCAR Winston Cup champion with team owner Raymond Beadle, inching out The Intimidator by 12 points.

After an 11-year separation, Wallace joined up again with Roger Penske in 1991, now as an established winner. His best years in the victory category came in 1993 and 1994, when he logged 18 wins in 61 starts over the two seasons. At the end of the 1996 season, Wallace won the inaugural Suzuka Thunder 100, a special non-points event held in Suzuka, Japan.

Wallace is undoubtedly one of the hottest stars in Winston Cup racing, having won at least one race in every season since 1986. He constantly demands more and more perfection from his crew. With Roger Penske, a longtime motorsports magnate who has enjoyed much success in Indy car racing, Wallace knows the chemistry is always there for success. Over a 17-year period, Wallace has collected 54 Winston Cup victories, 36 of them with Penske's organization. Now, all Wallace wants is more wins and at least one more Winston Cup championship before he someday turns his attention to other business ventures.

"We've had a few races slip away over the years for one reason or another," Wallace says. "But I know I've got 54 wins in record books and a championship in 1989 that I'm proud of. I'd like to get a few more wins and another championship before I stop driving."

Top Left: Wallace enjoys the cheers he receives at Bristol Motor Speedway in August 1998. He often admits that Bristol is one of his favorite tracks. **Top Right:** Wallace speeds along the concrete at Rockingham early in the 2002 season. **Right:** Wallace is in a familiar pose behind the controls of the Penske Racing Ford at New Hampshire in 1997.

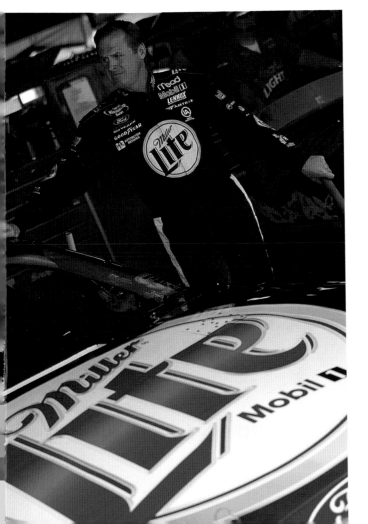

Above: Wallace makes a pit stop at Sears Point Raceway in California, a track where he earned victories in 1990 and again in 1996. Left: Wallace enjoys a spare moment in the garage area at Dover in June 2001. The 1989 Winston Cup Champion would love to have another taste of the title before he retires. Right: Wallace raises his arms in victory after taking the checkered flag at Bristol Motor Speedway in March 2000. It was Wallace's 53rd career win.

MICHAEL WALTRIP

15

Born:
April 30, 1963
Owensboro, Kentucky

Height: 6-5

Weight: 210 lbs

Sponsor
NAPA
Make
Chevrolet

Michael Waltrip is quick to tell you that stock cars aren't his only racing passion. The Owensboro, Kentucky, native has entered both the Boston Marathon and the Tampa Marathon. But it's in the NASCAR arena where his greatest talents lie, and like his teammate Kenny Wallace, Waltrip certainly knows how to hold court in any garage area.

The younger brother of three-time Winston Cup champion Darrell Waltrip, Michael is probably best known for his victory in the 2001 Daytona 500, in the 462nd start of a career dating back to 1985. The victory will forever be overshadowed by the death of Dale Earnhardt on the final lap—ironically, Waltrip was driving a Chevrolet owned by Earnhardt. He was in the lead, two positions ahead of the legend when the fatal crash occurred.

Waltrip returned to Daytona in July of that year and finished second to DEI teammate Dale Earnhardt Jr. in the 400-mile event. Waltrip now has over 500 starts in a career that also includes 21 top fives, 85 top 10s, and 2 pole positions. Waltrip captured a second career victory in 2002, and once again the trophy was earned at the famous Daytona International Speedway. The win in the Pepsi 400 that July supplied Waltrip brought encouragement for continued success with DEI.

In 2003, Waltrip scored his second career Daytona 500 in a rain-shortened event. He followed that win by taking the checkered flag at Talladega Superspeedway in October to help the DEI cars dominate those two tracks.

""Remember this: Dale Earnhardt was the best at Daytona and Talladega, and he knew that to be the best, you had to have the best cars," Waltrip says. "When he

NASCAR Winston Cup Career Statistics

Year	Races	Wins	Top 5s	Top 10s	Poles	Total Points	Final Standing	Winnings
1985	5	0	0	0	0	395	49th	$9,540
1986	28	0	0	0	0	2,853	19th	$108,767
1987	29	0	0	1	0	2,840	20th	$205,370
1988	29	0	1	3	0	2,949	18th	$240,400
1989	29	0	0	5	0	3,067	18th	$249,233
1990	29	0	5	10	0	3,251	16th	$395,507
1991	29	0	4	12	2	3,254	15th	$440,812
1992	29	0	1	2	0	2,825	23rd	$410,545
1993	30	0	0	5	0	3,291	17th	$529,923
1994	31	0	2	10	0	3,512	12th	$706,426
1995	31	0	2	8	0	3,601	12th	$898,338
1996	31	0	1	11	0	3,535	14th	$1,182,811
1997	32	0	0	6	0	3,173	18th	$1,138,599
1998	32	0	0	5	0	3,340	17th	$1,508,680
1999	34	0	1	3	0	2,974	29th	$1,701,160
2000	34	0	1	1	0	2,792	27th	$1,689,421
2001	36	1	3	3	0	3,159	24th	$3,411,644
2002	36	1	4	10	0	3,985	14th	$2,829,180
2003	36	2	8	11	0	3,934	15th	$4,463,485
Totals	570	4	33	106	2	58,764		$22,119,841

Michael Waltrip pushes his Dale Earnhardt Inc. Chevrolet to top speed around Richmond International Speedway in Virginia in May 2002.

started DEI, he made sure that everyone understood that he would have the best restrictor-plate cars. He was going to have cars that were faster than everyone else's, to give the drivers a chance to win. That was his signature at DEI. We're going to do whatever it takes to have the best program. He left his fingerprints all over DEI when he left us, and we just understand that it is our job to continue to execute and perform and build the type of equipment that he would be proud of. Dale is gone, but he is such a presence at our shop, and a presence when it comes to plate racing."

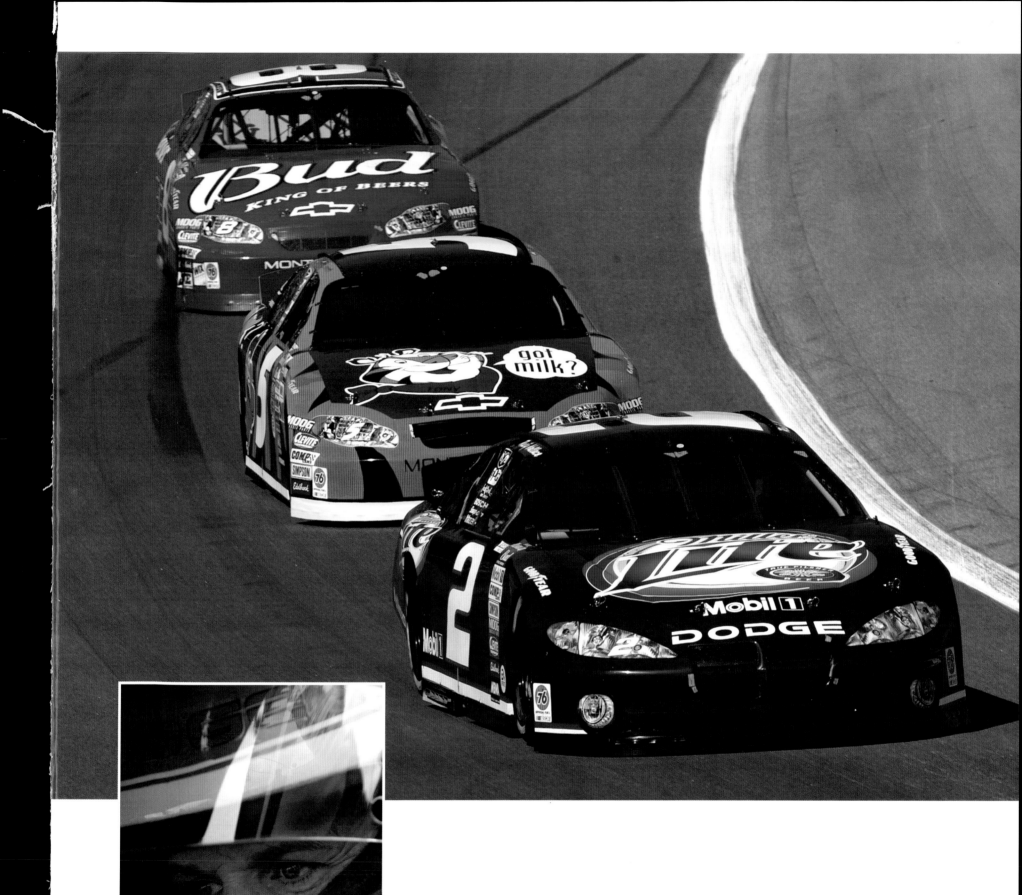